MW00615519

PUG RULES

Pug Rules

◪ WILLOW CREEK PRESS®

Published by Willow Creek Press, Inc.
P.O. Box 147, Minocqua, Wisconsin 54548

Photo Credits:
p5 © Juniors Bildarchiv/agefotostock.com; p8 © John Daniels/ardea.com/agefotostock.com;
p11 © Beate Zoellner/agefotostock.com; p12 © Colin Anderson/agefotostock.com; p15 © Zoonar/Stefan Ernst/agefotostock.com;
p19 © Tierfotoagentur/I. Pitsch/agefotostock.com; p20 © Juniors Bildarchiv/agefotostock.com; p23 © GCShutter/iStock;
p24 © Close Encounters of the Furry Kind/Kimball Stock; g27 © Mark McQueen/Kimball Stock; p28 © Terry J Alcorn/iStock;
p32 © retales botijero/iStock; p35 © H Schmidt-Roeger/agefotostock.com; p36 © C Mrazovic/agefotostock.com;
p39 © Juniors Bildarchiv/agefotostock.com; p40 © Tierfotoagentur/J. Hutfluss/agefotostock.com;
p43 © Tierfotoagentur/D. Jakob/agefotostock.com; p44 © Beate Zoellner/D. Jakob/agefotostock.com;
p47 © Juniors Bildarchiv/agefotostock.com;p48 © Juniors Bildarchiv/agefotostock.com;
p51 © H Schmidt-Roeger/agefotostock.com; p59 © Juniors Bildarchiv/agefotostock.com; p60 © C Mrazovic/agefotostock.com;
p63 © Tierfotoagentur/Y. Janetzek/agefotostock.com; p64 © Doreen Zorn/imageBROKER/agefotostock.com;
p67 © Iza Lyson/imageBROKER/agefotostock.com; p68 © SuperflyImages/iStock;
p71 © Jean-Michel Labat/ardea.com/agefotostock.com; p72 © Juniors Bildarchiv/agefotostock.com;
p75 © Juniors Bildarchiv/agefotostock.com; p76 © Miltonh09/iStock; p81 © MGStockPhotography/iStock;
p83 © FavoreStudio/iStock; p84 © nimis69/iStock; p88 © John Daniels/ardea.com/agefotostock.com;
p91 © Tierfotoagentur/K. L,hrs/agefotostock.com; p95 © Ben Robson/agefotostock.com;

Printed in China

DETERMINATION

Perseverance, secret of all triumphs.

— *Victor Hugo*

I'm good enough, I'm smart enough,
and doggone it, people like me.

—*Stuart Smalley*

Success seems to be largely
a matter of hanging on
after others have let go.

– William Feather

What counts is not necessarily the size of the dog
in the fight—it's the size of the fight in the dog.

—*General Dwight D. Eisenhower*

JOYFUL

All animals, except man, know that the
principal business of life is to enjoy it.

—*Samuel Butler*

Contentment is natural wealth.

—Socrates

...joy delights in joy.

—*William Shakespeare*

Sometimes your joy is the source of your smile, but sometimes your smile can be the source of your joy.

—*Thich Nhat Hanh*

We know nothing of tomorrow; our business
is to be good and happy today.

—*Sydney Smith*

To get the full value of joy
you must have someone
to divide it with.

—*Mark Twain*

CLOWNish

Dogs laugh, but they laugh with their tails.

—*Max Forrester Eastman*

The great pleasure of a dog is that you may make a fool of yourself with him and not only will he not scold you, but he will make a fool of himself too.

—*Samuel Butler*

Dogs don't mind being
photographed in
compromising situations.

—*Elliott Erwitt*

Be weird. Be random. Be who you are. Because you never know who would love the person you hide.

—*C.S. Lewis*

PATIENT

To know how to wait is the great secret of success.

—*Joseph Marie de Maistre*

Patience is the art of hoping.

—Luc de Clapiers

Adopt the pace of nature:
her secret is patience.

—*Ralph Waldo Emerson*

Don't cross the bridge
till you come to it.

—*Henry Wadsworth Longfellow*

DESIRE

The starting point of all achievement is desire.

—*Napoleon Hill*

The thirst of desire is never
filled, nor fully satisfied.

—*Marcus Tullius Cicero*

Is it not strange, that desire should so many years outlive performance.

—*William Shakespeare*

Obstacles do not block the path,
they are the path.

—Unknown

iNTELLiGENT

The dog has an enviable mind. It remembers the nice things in life and quickly blots out the nasty.

—*Barbara Woodhouse*

Intellectuals solve problems. Geniuses prevent them.

—*Albert Einstein*

Intelligence is the ability
to adapt to change.

—*Stephen Hawking*

Weak people revenge. Strong people forgive.
Intelligent people ignore.

—*Unknown*

CURiouS

A sense of curiosity is nature's
original school of education.

—*Smiley Blanton*

Millions saw the apple fall,
but Newton was the
one who asked why.

—*Bernard Baruch*

I have no special talents. I am only passionately curious.

—*Albert Einstein*

Curiosity will conquer fear even
more than bravery will.

—*James Stephens*

Curiosity is the engine
of achievement.

—*Ken Robinson*

The cure for boredom is curiosity.
There is no cure for curiosity.

—*Dorothy Parker*

HUMBLE

Whoever loves becomes humble.

—*Sigmund Freud*

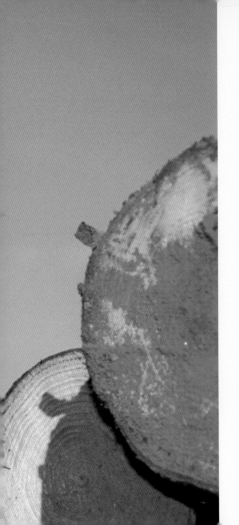

The higher we are placed, the more humbly we should walk.

—*Marcus Tullius Cicero*

Believe in yourself! Have faith in your abilities! Without a humble but reasonable confidence in your own powers you cannot be successful or happy.

—*Norman Vincent Peale*

The biggest challenge after success
is shutting up about it.

—*Criss Jami*

Loyal

There is no faith which has never yet been broken,
except that of a truly faithful dog.

—*Konrad Lorenz*

Loyalty means nothing
unless it has at its heart
the absolute principle
of self-sacrifice.

—*Woodrow T. Wilson*

The only people I owe my loyalty to are those who never made me question theirs.

—*Unknown*

Respect is earned. Honesty is appreciated.
Love is gained and loyalty is returned.

—*Criss Jami*

AFFECTIONATE

Always hold your head up, but be careful to
keep your nose at a friendly level.

—*Max L. Forman*

Dogs love company. They
place it first on their
short list of needs.

—*J.R. Ackerley*

We are shaped and fashioned by what we love.

—*Johann Wolfgang von Goethe*

No act of kindness, no matter how small, is ever wasted.

—*Aesop*

Little friends may prove great friends.

—*Aesop*